Touch the Dead

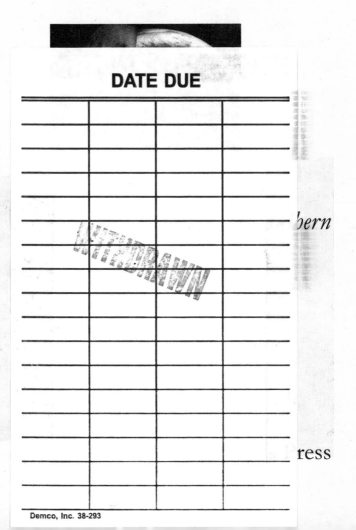

DATE DUE

bern

ress

Library and Archives Canada Cataloguing in Publication

Mulhern, Mary Ann
    Touch the dead / Mary Ann Mulhern.

Poems.
ISBN 0-88753-415-5

I. Title.

PS8576.U415T68 2006   C811'.6   C2006-900641-5

Cover Design: Maryszka Clovis

Published by Black Moss Press, 2450 Byng Road, Windsor, Ontario N8W 3E8. Black Moss Press books are distributed by LitDistco, and all orders should be directed there.

Black Moss acknowledges the generous support of the Canada Council for the Arts and the Ontario Arts Council for its publishing program.

With special thanks to Bernie Clement and DaimlerChrylser for their support in supplying transportation for our research.

Le Conseil des Arts | The Canada Council
du Canada | for the Arts

ONTARIO ARTS COUNCIL
CONSEIL DES ARTS DE L'ONTARIO

Introduction

I grew up in the cemetery house bordering Holy Angels' Cemetery in St. Thomas, Ontario. This created a unique landscape for a curious child whose worldview came from deep graves covered with flowers and tears.

My father, an Irish immigrant, was the cemetery caretaker. He dug graves, cut grass, planted trees and flowers, and kept a careful map. His labour was a work of mercy, *to bury the dead*.

Mourners, undertakers and priests seemed to recognize "the gravedigger" as a man who confronted death in layers of soil. Perhaps he uncovered answers the living needed from the dead, those whom he placed in the fecundity of earth, from which they might be reborn to rise and speak again.

Funerals and poems both have feelings, images, voices, and stories with levels of colour, and meaning, and the consolation of language. In *Touch the Dead*, poems present the changing perspectives of a young child who becomes a sensitive adolescent and, finally, a woman whose experiences with death gradually reveal mortality, all the burdens of grief and love.

Acknowledgments

I wish to recognize the talent and craft of Marty Gervais and his editorial team for their insightful and intelligent attention to these poems. These include Stephen Pender, Lindsey Bannister, Maryszka Clovis, Jamie Kathryn Gaunt, Laurie Gibson, Stefanie Helbich, Caitlin McNamara, James Prophet, Marissa Reaume, Lindsey Rivait, Melanie Santarossa, Devon Stinchcombe, Sonia Sulaiman, Brendan Thomas, Meighan Topolnicki, Ryan Turgeon, Lindsay Turner, Ben Van Dongen, Michael Wheeler.

Also, I want to thank my family and friends for their continued encouragement in this endeavor, especially my brothers, Mike and Pat. Susan McMaster guided me in the early stages of this work. Her suggestions have been extremely valuable.

Some poems from *Touch the Dead* were previously published in *The Windsor Review; Room of One's Own; Tower; Windfall*, an anthology; and *Reginaweese*, an on-line publication.

The Mourner's Dance, by Katherine Ashenburg, was a resource for "Conclamatio Mortis," "'Til Death," and "When a Child is Taken."

Also by Mary Ann Mulhern:
The Red Dress, Black Moss Press, 2003.

To my parents, Patrick and Ann,
who offered gifts of life.

My father often spoke of a wealthy man in Ireland who owned a magnificent estate named Rockaway. It overlooked the Irish Sea. Before he died, he repeated over and over, "Oh Rockaway, Rockaway, how can I ever leave you?"

Table of Contents

In this house words and tears
have a place
My father is a man
who puts shovel to soil
whose sweat bleeds into clay and rock
He knows the depths of grief
feels it in his hands
climbing up from graves

Cemetery Games

I grew up in a cemetery
watched my father measure out a grave
played hide and seek with angels
Tombstones were my books
names, dates, unanswered prayers
smooth carve of pink granite
cool against my skin

I hid behind white marble
peeked out at coffins and graves
Death could never find me
Death could never dare
spell my name

Purple and White

Today the cemetery is silent
Freshly mown grass
lies in neat rows
around crumbled stone
My father plants summer flowers
yellow, orange and red
He refuses purple and white
seeded colours of death
full blooms an omen
deep harvest of graves

Strawberries

My mother grows strawberries
watches them spread
across the earth
always fearful
young shoots might
run across sunken graves
wrap around an unnamed cross
arouse hunger among the dead

In late June
my brothers and I
help her fill small
woven baskets
Bruised berries are eaten
by birds, crushed like snakes
left bloodied on vines
red pulp festered with worms
Things that happen to berries
to the unchosen
those left behind

Root Cellar

My father digs a root cellar
deeper than a grave
Earth takes back her harvest
apples, potatoes, turnips and squash
Seeds still alive
like a woman whose
buried children turned to ghosts
while they still had breath and eyes
to beg for sustenance
Apples for a Sunday pie
potatoes for a stew
turnips and squash steaming in a pot
Sweet resurrection

Empty Closet

On a table in the cemetery house
Mrs. Finn unfolds dresses
bright moments from her daughter's life
rainbows over lace
birthday parties every year
a first communion bride
buried in a satin box

She holds blue organdy
asks me to try it on
A mirror brings her Emily back
slender ghost
held in blue shades of light
Mrs. Finn embraces me
holds my kiss on her lips
weeps for her child
silent fade of hope

Heavy Loads

Every Monday morning
my mother fills the wringer washer
soap, hot water, a cup of smelly bleach
Begins load after load of clothes
Feeds dripping sheets, shirts, towels, underwear
through a wringer mean enough to take fingers
crush a woman's hands to useless stumps of pain
She carries heavy baskets into the grassy yard
sings her Gaelic songs, hangs clothes line after line

Sudden winds turn white sheets into troubled spirits
struggling to escape flimsy wooden pins
fallen lines, loads of dirty clothes
a lonely cemetery house
on a gravel road

Under the Dead Woman's Dress

An undertaker in a long coat
leaves an oak coffin in the winter mausoleum
until my father can open a grave
He says there's a woman inside the casket

My little brother wants to know
what's under the dead woman's dress
He goes alone into the dead house
climbs inside a wheelbarrow
runs small fingers along the polished lid
until a hidden latch clicks
The coffin opens with a whoosh
a sound he's heard on Hallowe'en
The dead woman's dress is heavy black
her hair a ghostly white
all her braids undone
Large glasses shine like open eyes
Huge hands clutch dark beads
curve like claws
ready to reach out
snatch a bad little boy
pull him inside
shut the lid

Poison Berries

In my fingers, berries break like hearts
juices spatter like fresh blood
cover my hands with shame

My brothers beg me to run home
to scrub my skin clean
before my throat swells
chokes me into a corpse
laid out in a coffin
airless, lined with white

Finding Out

I'm not yet five
My brother reads names
on marble stones
tells me
someday I too
will die

His words,
the first shovel of earth
hitting a pine box
end my childhood
open before me
a single grave

I'm not yet five
Someday I too
will die

Grasping Purple

Behind the cemetery
a deep ravine slides down to Kettle Creek
I've wandered past thickened roots
searching for hidden violets
velvet in my hands

Above me, the ground shakes
air thickens with bellows and shouts
the farmer's bull running wild
desperate men wielding ropes

No one knows I'm here
A five-year old girl
grasping purple flowers
waving a colour of death
before the trample of feet
crush of bone
scream of blood

Firstborn Son

My youngest brother follows my father
along the cemetery path
My father tells him to play
to run home when funeral cars
pass through gilded gates

Paddy Jo makes up a game
with mossy stones of death
skipping and running
loudly calling names
John Paul O'Neil
Mary Louise Ryan
Michael Vincent Bruce
until he finds a small marker
reads his own name
Patrick Joseph Mulhern

A baby born years ago
buried in the sorrow of Irish grief
reaching through earth and grass
crying to his brother
The one who steals his life

When Marble Turns Warm

Our house is haunted
by lawn ornaments
gravestones waiting for names and dates
Ideal Monuments for sale

Like summer ghosts
my brothers and I wait
on the wooden porch
pray for people
to honour their dead with marble
money for warm coats and boots
enough coal in the cellar
to burn through February frosts
deeper than death

For I Have Sinned

I lied to my mother once
made faces at my brothers three times
ate candy in Lent five times
forgot morning prayers twice

Sins I must tell
in a darkened box
Scarlet stains on my soul
turn to flame
red glow of fear

Bless me Father

Touch the Dead

In the funeral home
my mother kneels before a coffin
kisses her friend
says you should touch the dead
they are not lost to love
a language warm as breath
taken in from birth

I see my mother's eyes
bright shine of tears
I want to grasp her hand
feel warm fingers joined with mine
run from this red-lipped corpse
before it kisses me

Cold Flowers

My friend Linda is nine
her little sister asleep
in an open coffin
near the silent piano
thin body dressed
in soft satin
blue eyes closed to light
pale lips shaped in
unspoken words
whispers of play

In Linda's bedroom
frost cuts flowers on glass
Scents from a holy candle
flame red in her throat
All through the night
Linda listens for a piano
small fingers on keys
white and black

Storms

Inside warm rooms of the cemetery house
my brothers and I look through frosted windows
Electric wires hang from poles
long black serpents
ready to strike
Trees around the cemetery
bend like glass sculptures
fragile as old soldiers
afraid of storms
white signs of death

We drink hot tea
stay behind wooden doors
away from deep fields of snow
hidden graves ready to open
wherever we step

A Better Place

Like a small white ghost
a casket rises slowly
from a sunken grave
A child whose sleep
has been disturbed
Summer storms seep into pine
soft bones of peace

After decades of darkness
a grandfather asks to see his angel
to touch her long red hair
soft veil still bright as sunset
in an amber sky
as if she's waiting for morning

Lux aeterna
light from eternity

Roots

A black monument
shadows a grave
of many years
John Fields
husband and father

Like dancers on ice
winged seeds spin through air
find fertile soil
beside his grave
Roots spread, gather, entwine
take hold around marble
like his children holding hands
in a circle
white markers
etched with names
called by angels

one by one

To Save Him

On the heated day
of our school picnic
a boy swims
in a milky pond
deeper than he knew

Lunch in the wooden pavilion
turns cold as we gather
on a grassy bank
each of us alone
floating above silence

Pale-faced nuns finger
black beads
listen for whispers
of salvation
escape of breath from waters
turning dark

Divers search with lights
no words
not even his name
this boy who is lost
until they lift him
whited skin over bone
Small frightened ghost
whispering across channels of death
asking us to save him
a seat on the bus

Flashes of Hope

Driven by spirits of whiskey and gin
a car knocks against cemetery gates
misses a turn
smashes through glassy centres of night

Fear lights every neighbour's house
My father pulls on overalls
runs along the cemetery path
bright circles from his railroad lamp
small redemption for blood
on the road
inside a car
all over a flowered dress
Sounds of a siren draw close
Flashes of hope end in silence
dark carriage of death

In the morning
I search for ghosts
sudden rise of souls
from stones on a gravel road
I find a pink shoe
under strawberry leaves
high heel, shiny straps, open toe
A Cinderella shoe worn in the dance
lost in the speed of midnight
every stroke of magic gone

What Really Happens?

The mausoleum
two rooms of grey cement blocks
On a low shelf
a box of brown, brittle bones
mixed up like forgotten toys at home

Fear of these bones
leaves my hands
My fingers grasp a skull
stripped bare of flesh
bright cells of memory
I pull death out of these bones
probe secrets
from hollow mouth and eyes
I want a name, a sex, a face
a time when strong bones
walked, played, skipped and danced

I put the puzzle together
see bones of life
joined in death
What happens when the heart
runs out of beats?
When the spirit separates from bones?
Are couplings of love
forgotten in marrow
left alone to die?

In my hands
I could swear
a skull looks back
smiles

Christmas Message

In grade four
Mrs. Quinn asks us
to draw names
make Christmas cards
greetings of peace
A crumpled card
pinned to cork opens
reveals my name
smudged in wax crayon
beside a black snowman
a barren tree
The snowman sends a sneer
the tree spits out needles
dark whispers of malice
that strike, bite, and sting

His Heart They Said

Uncle John visits from New York
distant city of subways and crowds
He brings his friend Mike
a man who slaves on Manhattan's docks
unloading darkened hulls, weighted ships of trade
Mike reaches out to take my hand
I see him then, his pain held inside boxes
tied with ropes my small hand cannot ease
my whispered welcome cannot release
At ten years of age I do not know
he mourns a young wife and child
blown into graves by a Belfast bomb
their ghosts crowding into loneliness
shrouded by his smile

Within a year a letter tells us Mike is dead
Doctors blame his heart
I knew there was damage
whole oceans of loss
more than any heart could hold

Godmother

Mary Egan, my godmother
swept the rectory clean
cooked hot meals for priests
lived her life in small, separate rooms

Sunday evenings she changed from invisible white
into a flowered dress
walked miles to the cemetery house
spoke to my parents in Gaelic tones
joined them for tea and cake
I could see loneliness emptied from her painted cup
fortune of bitter leaves left unread
beneath clear amber light

Our house became a cottage
close to Mayo's Sea
where candles burned like vigils
melted silence into hope
long after dark

I turned in my sleep
saw my godmother
return to a locked rectory
Rooms with high windows
solitary priests, single beds
covered with white sheets
needing to be stripped
scrubbed clean in Monday's wash

Tramp

In musty August heat
a man with no name
knocks on our screen door
He's younger than most
who wander gravel roads
hair the colour of hay
smell of barns on wrinkled clothes

I help my mother make a sandwich
yesterday's ham on thick Irish bread
warm tea to soften thirst
His hunger fills our kitchen
spreads over the table
like dust from bones
broken, disconnected from flesh and blood
hollow spaces left to ache
in the mean, grey set of years

My father gives him a day's work
filling a grave, cutting grass
pulling weeds around tilted stones
He accepts some apples, a few dollars
a clean cotton shirt

In fear of night
he walks down an unmapped road
My mother says the dead go with him
guide him in the dark

Halfway Down a Grave

Sometimes when my father
is halfway down a grave
a pilgrim comes through cemetery gates
seeking answers
from a priest with a shovel in his hands
bloodred clay around his feet
A man who makes maps of the dead
names, dates of birth and death
all the words between
lost or forgotten
White pages of silence
spread across the cemetery
ghosts with stories to tell
Only a gravedigger to listen
to see the imprint of sunken graves
crush of coffins
on bones over hearts
gone hollow with grief

Telling the Truth

In first year high school
new kids from tobacco farms
ride yellow buses into class
Some ask
what my father does
I tell them
he digs graves
cuts grass around marble monuments
in the cemetery
beside our house

They say I'm telling lies
trying to make fools
of farm kids
My father doesn't dig graves
I don't live
in a red-brick house
surrounded by ghosts

I should have told them
my father is a doctor
dressed in white
who pulls babies into dawn
wailing with life
A man whose work
is about beginnings

I should have told lies
I should have made fools of them

When Angels Step Down

On hot summer nights
far from rules of heaven
sins of earth
angels step down
from carved marble and stone
They long for hearts
heated blood of flesh
bodies without the weight of wings
carnal love they can feel
open lips to kiss
enter into paradise

Requiem for Madness

Sister Ruth stands on a wooden stool
directs us in requiem
mass for a woman
from the asylum

Her body lies inside a coffin
draped in funeral black
her name already dust
on empty parish pews
A virgin veiled in blue
steps on a serpent who never dies
Plaster saints bear white flowers
blossoms turned to stone
Schoolgirls in navy pleats
chant *dies irae*
make notes of Friday's dance
what colour to wear
scent to splash between breasts

Chrysalis in the Snow

No one knew Arnie
He was a pale chrysalis, wings too weak
too wet for colours of flight
Other boys watched him curl
behind his translucent weave of fear

A teacher said Arnie could draw
castles that soared beyond silence
into spaces lit by stars
She wanted him to write their stories
to sign his name

No one knew Arnie
a shy boy who walked away from a yellow bus
slipped into white drifts of death
thin arms outstretched
as if he could fly

Rations of War

My mother has numbered coupons
flour
sugar
coffee
butter
meat
Staples of life rationed
portioned into small brown bags
tied with string
passed out like bullets to a soldier
enough for today

Tomorrow is another battlefield
a ruined farm
livestock, crops
plowed under armies and tanks
Tomorrow is another battlefield
dry yield of weeds and bones
September harvest sprayed with blood
Tomorrow is another battlefield
seeds of peace
buried with men
who'll never come home

Trace of Bones

An only son traces
his father's grave
on the cemetery map
Finds his own name
penciled on ruled paper
Six feet of earth
dug deep into bones
hollow spaces
beginning to ache
The only connection
broken until now
words spoken to a man
who buries the dead

When I was young
I disgraced my father's name
spent time in jail
For years we didn't speak
He asked for me
in his last days
I stayed away
Waited 'til he died
like a man in a prison
alone in a cell

Fabric of Salvation

Rosary beads like black eyes on a chain
Sister Thomasine walks
between rows of wooden desks
holds up a cloth scapular
blessed by a holy priest
fabric of salvation
worn on our breasts
safe from Satan's grasp

Sister Thomasine tells the story
of a teenaged girl who danced close
seduced her boyfriend to sin
A girl who drowned in a forbidden lake
tangled scapular found floating
far from a body washed ashore
lifeline of her eternal soul, lost

Slowly, silence fills the room
none of us can breathe

Churchyard Tale

Two hundred years ago
Charlotte Benns was buried
in a satin bridal gown
Her bridegroom desired the ruby ring
he'd placed on her pale finger
When night spilled over earth
he entered her tomb
found her eyes open
hungry body awake
like a vampire
wearing a ruby ring
facets burning with clarity
bright, red as blood

Bird of Fire

My father saves for airfare
to Ireland's voices and tears
Monsignor Martin is afraid
a bird of fire will devour my father
spit his bones into an Atlantic grave
where he can never rest
never rise up
never save his children from storms

If a Shadow Stumbles

A man down the road
washed his rusted car
took garbage to the curb
raked leaves into piles

Climbed his attic steps
thoughts drained of hope
His children said he fell
from a wobbly wooden chair
a long cord tangled
around his life
a shadow stumbling
in the dark

His children know
the attic is a tomb
inside their house
a space where none of them
can hide
Some steps are missing
Any child could fall

Roses for Love

Lina owns a small flower shop
close to a church
She arranges flowers better than life
removes ruined roots and leaves
chooses blossoms ready to open
roses for love, lilies for loss, orchids for joy
Lina knows all the long Latin names
like a litany of saints
rosa majalis, lilium candidium, neofinetia
petals delicate as a virgin's skin
red as a martyr's blood
fragrance remembered as gifts
rosa majalis, roses for love
lilium landidium, lilies for loss
neofinetia, orchids for joy
A look, a smile, a kiss
redolent of that one embrace held
long past goodbye

Ego te absolvo

Jack Finn sold us his wife's piano
said it made him lonely
to see it silent, beautiful
Music and love locked inside
waiting for her touch

Years later he remarried
a woman who'd been divorced
lived in grievous sin
Days before death
Jack begged for a priest
one who never came
to anoint eyes, ears, nose, mouth and tongue
Holy oils, holy words
ego te absolvo

My father opened a grave
in Potter's field
unconsecrated ground
far from angels carved in cemetery gates
Jack's name marked on a folded map
his piano his only benediction
So many keys to paradise

Circle of Flames

In a harsh winter
frost bites deeply
into cemetery ground
My father burns old tires
all night
on a gravesite
he'll open tomorrow

In the worry of dreams
I see a circle of flames
smell oily rubber
mixed with tar

Death hides
in twists and turns
of smoke
Leaves black layers
of dust on lace curtains
in my house

Like a Prisoner

In the morning
my father removes blackened ruin of tires
breaks frozen ground with a pick-axe
He works like a prisoner
condemned to hard labour
rough hands reddened with cold

This grave goes too deep
leverages layers of pain
in a gravedigger's soul
This grave could be his
could fill his lungs
drag him into the pulley of ropes
lowering a pine box
into the dirge of January winds

When a Child is Taken

Alice Reeves lives down the road
in white pain of winter
her baby girl is born
Blue silence of death
covered with linen
hidden in a casket
buried in a day

Alice buys a porcelain doll
real enough to breathe
She burns a candle blessed by God
christens her baby in water from eternity
names her daughter Sarah
enfolds her in woven flowers
opened into lace
every stitch a gift
delicate as life

Alice buries her porcelain child
with a lullaby
fresh roses, ivy and columbine
a place where Sarah belongs
where she can sleep

Missing Flowers

My father lowers a widow's coffin
into a box made of pine
her body and soul released
from the asylum for the insane

January winds
move her spirit
and name her children
one by one
Where are they?
White blossoms spilled
from her womb
lost in snow
scattered in cities
in houses along country roads
none of them here
to embrace a mother
pregnant with grief

They've grown into wild flowers
fragile threads of roots
left to rot
in frozen ground

'Til Death

In the long, slow linger
of shadow before light
Sean Conlin struggles until the end
His wife closes her husband's eyes
kisses his forehead, whispers goodbye
Kate Conlin opens windows and doors
covers every mirror in black
stops all the clocks

Sean's spirit is here
restless, angry about his fate
If he sees a pale reflection in the mirror
he may stay, draw his widow
into glass cold as a corpse
haunt her with marriage vows

Signals

When the last mourner
passes through cemetery gates
my father begins
filling the grave
he opened only yesterday
Sounds of earth
heavy with grief
cover a lifetime
a man my father knew
in railroad years
when they switched signals
in frozen midnight yards
felt the thunder of trains
fire of sparks on rusted rails
like the laboured beating of hearts
ending somewhere close to home

Orphans

A widow stands beside a winter grave
Her children mill like sheep
in the silent freeze of fear
their father sinking into darkness
their lives buried with him
slow starve of poverty
slaves on summer farms
searching soil and sky for their father
his love like silk on corn
his spirit rising up to feed them

Gathering Worry

On days when
the furnace pushed heat
through a dusty grate
in the hall
soft grains of morning
brought me downstairs
to a naked bulb
dangling over oilcloth
gathering worry
around wavering light
My father in overalls
stirring his cup
waiting
to taste black coffee
My mother fading
into her housedress
turning potatoes and eggs
in an iron pan

The radio spilling out news
bad weather

Phone Call

Graves, marble stones
coffins lowered with flowers and prayers
never did open death
It was a phone call
There's been an accident
Your friend died at 2 pm
First measure of grief
an hour within a day, a month, a year
an exact time I can believe
like your name
inscribed in dark granite
every letter cut
deep enough to keep
you in your grave
to keep me
for hours, days, months, years
breathing in your place

Something Left Undone

Colleen's mother begs me to stay
In pale winter light
she tells the story of her daughter's death
over and over
searching with every word for dangling threads
something she's left undone
like a button that doesn't fit
an unraveled hem
a worn patch about to fray
something she can mend

I listen but cannot reach her
where she stands in the cemetery
measuring graves
wanting to trade places
tear open every seam of her daughter's shroud
sew herself in

Kept From Heaven

A young woman
weeps over the phone
Her baby died
in a winter crib
before waters of baptism
cleansed his newborn soul
A priest says
her son is in limbo
kept from heaven
healing warmth
of his mother's milk
filling her breasts
with pain

She wants my father
to bring her baby back
from shadows of earth
to open a white cradle
let her awaken her child
call him by name
offer him to God

Bearing Gifts

On the eve of Christmas
we pass through cemetery gates
Darkness weighs heavy as stone
footprints drift in snow
vanish without a trace
My niece holds a railroad lamp
circles of light on names
we have known
shadows of souls
who linger here

We find familiar graves
place a wreath
evergreen gathered from trees
branches still reaching out
scent of winter pine
like frankincense and myrrh

Dia di los Muertos

I'm tired of dark cemetery tales
haunted ghosts and ghouls
skeletons dancing in pale lunar light

I know the people
in this holy place
the family doctor
whose hands drove pain from flesh and bone
the neighbour who took pictures my father could send
across the sea
the woman down the road who sewed my dresses every year
the farmer who brought us meat, butter and eggs

I want to bring armfuls of orange blossoms
baskets of pomegranates, bottles of wine
burn a thousand candles to celebrate
a day of the dead
enter into their circle
call each of them by name
listen for an answer
their remembrance familiar
warm as breath

Likeness of a Nun

In her winter of mourning
a young widow combs long, dark hair
her husband's desire
spread over pillows
curled around his fingers
in tangled moments of play

She pulls every strand
in tight braids, like a nun
shears broken ends
cuts beauty into cold, celibate nights
shrouds her body in black
remains in the silence of her cloister
until a mirror reflects uneven growth
hair needing a softer shape
deeper tones of light

Conclamatio mortis

Petals covering a recent grave
flame red
like a funeral pyre
A young man in a hunting accident
early morning prey
moving in the fall of trees
a cocked rifle
one shot

Birds rise like angry spirits
wild disarray of wings
chaos of calls
Conclamatio mortis
loud report of death

Names

Forgotten in the deep carve of stone
remember smooth pages of life
signed birthday cards
forbidden love letters
invitations to weddings
diplomas from college
passports to London, Paris, Seville and Rome
Names passed on to children
who toss out cards, letters, diplomas and passports
in garbage bags at the dump
another grave
nameless

When Barbie Breaks

In the grocery store
an aging Barbie Doll
empties her cart
biscuits, tea, lemons and juice
She leans on the counter
long yellow hair pulled back
from a wide-eyed skull
tall, thin body covered in black
tiny waist cinched with safety pins
long skirt tattered like jeans
She carries a redwood cane
to keep her standing

I've seen her before
in another grocery line
felt the hunger she brings
whited skin over bones
corpse of a fantasy
limping to her grave

Warnings

One hour before light
the train awakens me
warning signals in early morning

Like suicide, a lament
tragic spirit of a young man
rising from distant tracks
in the mourn of a whistle
haunting my room

Glory

In early benediction of light
maybe God comes into the cemetery
seeking solitude from war
bombs heard in the universe
holy, holy, holy
A million prayers
exploding into grief
Sabbath dark as ash
raining on the sun

The dead understand silence
feel the blessing of God's peace
among the trees, grass, flowers and stone
nesting birds that call forth His song
their glory

Knowing

The grey morning my father
went to the hospital
he wore his long navy coat
and his good Sunday hat
The fine-stitched woolen coat
masked his mortal chill
and the dark fedora
hid the fear in his knowing eyes
shadowed his famine-white skin

And in the neon clinic glare
I saw my father naked
wailing at his birth
weeping at his death

Monument

In the cemetery
a priest points to trees
maple, oak, and elm
seeded by my father's hand
A living monument
for an ordinary man
with an ordinary name
reborn in eternal cycles
of earth and sky
root, branch, stem and bud
witness of a million leaves
in the turn of light

Resurrection

My father wanted his children
to rise up
He gave us wings
to lift us from the graveyard of his life
to leave forever
ground broken for death
gravel mixed into cement
vaults for coffins of oak
angels of stone praying
over forgotten bones

He gave us flight
bound into books
opening into eternities
each of us could choose

Mourning

My mother
sat beside my brother
watched him die
before her

This morning
she tries to dress
for his Requiem
wrinkled hands
shaking grey stockings
in her lap
Silence covers grief
when I help
with her clothes
pull thin arms
through woolen sleeves
As my mother dressed
her firstborn son
fine silk threads from her womb
woven into a white robe
worn on the day
he was baptized
named a child of God

A Leper's Bell

Cancer on my mother's face
radiant glow of burns
blisters rising from her heart
slow suffering of blood
on flowered pillows and sheets

She submits to doctors
white coats, white stares
Sterile probe of pain
My mother hears a distant bell
feels a white wound, a leprosy
too deep to clean, or heal, or bind

Skeleton

In the spooky glow of Hallowe'en
a skeleton jangles on a string
Children laugh, run away

Brittle bones hide beneath my wrinkled skin
They want to break through
show their missing teeth
grin into my mirror
like a child wearing a scary costume
she can throw away
tomorrow

Reading My Heart

Death hovers
over the marrow of my bones
slow sip of pain through transparent tubes
Long shine of needles
probe of neon light
gibberish blip of machines
reading my heart
pulsing script on a lighted screen
Electric lines that tell nothing
of me, an old woman
caught between hours of night
like a small bird
in the mouth of a gull
far from her mother's cries
swallowed in pieces
hope of feathered wings
scattered over snow

In Fear of Morning

I must go alone
to the cemetery
In the deep grave of night
even angels lose their way
Cold winds sprout long fingers, sharp nails
Early rains press down
slow strangle of breath
sounds of drowning, or weeping
I am afraid of morning
when light draws me closer
shouts my name

The Gravedigger's Shoulders

In a dream
my father and I
drink tea in a shop
Someone remembers him
as the caretaker of Holy Angels
asks to take his picture outside

I watch from a window
Sunlight exposes a ghost
an old man I've never seen
the gravedigger's shoulders
slack and thin
as if he's never held a shovel
lifted the weight of earth
smelled the heavy clay of grief

He stares into a bloodred eye
waits for his image
to appear from darkness
traces of who he is
shadows of who he was

Sudden rains ruin his suit
Cloth wrinkles like skin
close to bone
uncertain measure of life
I bring him inside
keep him warm
away from dark thunder
dangerous flashes of light

Preserves

Whispers of our cemetery house
rise from this empty space
Cellar shelves filled with my mother's
fruits and jams
strawberries, peaches, plums, and pears
Ripe colours preserved in sweet juices
Flavours sealed with heated wax
food to fill white bowls of winter
when graves push through snow
hungry for fevered bones
children whose lips have dried
like red fruit torn from trees
in the sudden turn of winds

Returning

When winter white
marks the innocence of death
the cemetery calls me closer
hides a name the same as mine
under the cold cover of snow

I look for a longneedled pine
above my parents' grave
Brown cones hang
like seeded fruit
stolen from Eden
fit the curve of my hand
as if they belong
as if they've come to stay

Afterlife

When I die, what will remain?

Will my spirit wander
these few rooms in search of breath?

Will my bones rebuild
in the womb of another race?

Will I be swaddled
in new songs, myths, and chants?
Struggle again with seeds of love
pressed from unyielding hands
of a distant God?

Or will my ashes scatter like words
carried by winds
whispers no one understands
no one wants to hear?

At the Table

The cemetery house
one eighty-eight gravel road
is gone

The spirit of the house
opens rooms in my mind
invites me into the kitchen
to my place at the wooden table
My mother is sifting flour
over apples in a pan
sorrow from her wrinkled brow
silent as apples under a knife
seeds of her life
in danger of drought
My mother knows how wind-driven storms
shift into death
how the kitchen window
lets in stones over graves
my father digs every day
his sweat traded
for a sack of flour
a bag of apples

Cemetery House

A skeleton now
windows and doors taken
spaces like eyes in a skull
two floors of papered rooms
left naked, ashamed of rain
Breath has turned to dust
Babies sleep in graves

Wind rises from the cellar
whistles through broken jars
remains of summer fruit